MAKE ROOMS LOOK PRETTIER OR ADD PIZAZZ WITH AN EXPERT'S BIG IDEAS FOR SMALL PRICES

UNDER $25—From stencil kits to creative shelving, "blackboard paint" for children's rooms and luscious lighting for pennies.

UNDER $50—From outdoor furniture indoors to terrific tables, beautiful baskets, and fabulous fabrics for walls and furniture.

UNDER $100—From hanging storage space to tatami mats, decorative fixtures, room dividers, canopy beds, and wonderful windows.

UNDER $200—From generous closets to elegant walls, mirrored ceilings, multilevel platforms, and a glamorous Hollywood bed.

UNDER $300—From trellis window treatments to posh Flokati rugs, a greenhouse, romantic bathrooms, and ornamental ceilings.

UNDER $500—From Shoji screens to luxurious fur rugs, marble table tops, overhead fans, and a sophisticated built-in bar.

AND MUCH, MUCH MORE!

KAREN FISHER has worked as decorating editor for *Cosmopolitan*, *Esquire*, and *American Home*. She is the successful author of *The Power Look at Home*, *A Man's Guide to Decorating*, and *Living for Today*.

RICHARD TOGLIA'S drawings have appeared in numerous home furnishing magazines, and he does a bi-monthly 6-page photofolio for *House Beautiful's Colonial Homes*. He has also illustrated several books.

QUICK FIX DECORATING IDEAS

by
Karen Fisher

Drawings by
Richard Toglia

Ⓟ

A PLUME BOOK

NEW AMERICAN LIBRARY

NEW YORK AND SCARBOROUGH, ONTARIO

NAL BOOKS ARE AVAILABLE AT QUANTITY DISCOUNTS
WHEN USED TO PROMOTE PRODUCTS OR SERVICES, FOR
INFORMATION PLEASE WRITE TO PREMIUM MARKETING DIVISION,
NEW AMERICAN LIBRARY, 1633 BROADWAY,
NEW YORK, NEW YORK 10019.

Cover photo: Elyse Lewin

Book designed by Julian Hamer

PLUME TRADEMARK REG. U.S. PAT. OFF. AND FOREIGN COUNTRIES
REGISTERED TRADEMARK—MARCA REGISTRADA
HECHO EN HARRISONBURG, VA., U.S.A.

SIGNET, SIGNET CLASSIC, MENTOR, PLUME, MERIDIAN,
and NAL BOOKS are published *in the United States*
by New American Library, 1633 Broadway,
New York, New York 10019, *in Canada* by
The New American Library of Canada Limited,
81 Mack Avenue, Scarborough, Ontario M1L 1M8

LIBRARY OF CONGRESS CATALOGING IN PUBLICATION DATA
Fisher, Karen.
   Quick fix decorating ideas.

   Includes index.
   1. Interior decoration. I. Toglia, Richard.
II. Title.
NK2115.F53   1984   747'.1   83-23775
ISBN 0-452-25519-8

First Printing, May, 1984

1 2 3 4 5 6 7 8 9

PRINTED IN THE UNITED STATES OF AMERICA

For Barbara Demaras, who has helped me through every move—including this one.
—*Karen Fisher*

For Andre Laporte, who was the first to suggest that I draw interiors. My thanks for initiating this project with Karen.
—*Richard Toglia*

Contents

Introduction

Four Walls . . .
Now What?

Most decorating books assume you want to start decorating from scratch—throw out your furniture, knock out the walls, and buy a few precious antiques—but unless you just came into an inheritance, you're probably more interested in improving on what you have at a price you can afford. That's what *Quick Fix Decorating Ideas* is about. *Quick Fix* ideas are straightforward and inexpensive. You'll be amazed by how easy it is to give a room a fresh, new look without spending a lot of time and money.

I've been the decorating editor of *Cosmopolitan, Esquire,* and *American Home,* and over the years, I've designed hundreds of apartments and houses and worked with some of America's top decorators. Most of these places were successful and glamorous because the rooms contained one or two great ideas. This book shows the best of those ideas.

We've illustrated many of the ideas so that you can visualize them in your own room. You might also take this book along when you're shopping for materials. The clerks at lumber yards and hardware stores are usually more helpful when they can see what your project is.

It's important to know what a project will cost before you start, so I've chaptered the book by cost. However, you should still price a project out completely before beginning. The costs in the book were my costs on the projects, and sometimes I overpaid for materials, and sometimes I got a great bargain; occasionally I was able to do the work myself where someone else would have needed a carpenter or an electrician.

There are many easy projects here. However, some of the projects do involve knowledge of carpentry and electrical knowledge. If you want to rewire a lamp, or build a bookcase, you should turn to the bibliography at the end of the book, and then take the time to read up on the skills you will need.

I hope that you'll use *Quick Fix* for years, and that you'll find dozens of ideas here to make your home a more wonderful place in which to live.

—*Karen Fisher*

Chapter One
First Decisions

I once asked a top New York designer how he would decorate his own house if he only had $250 to spend.

"I'd invest the whole amount in a paint job," he said.

"But what if your furniture was old? Wouldn't you want new slipcovering instead?" I asked.

"Nobody would notice my furniture if the walls were a beautiful color."

When professionals approach a budget job, their priority is making changes that will show. Walls, floors, and windows are the elements that give a room its style. When decorating, these are your top priorities. So we'll start with them first.

Painting

Step One: Choosing a Color Scheme

How do you know which colors to choose? This is one of the trickiest questions in decorating, and the answer will ultimately depend as much on your personality as on the room you are decorating. Here are some starting points:

• Select a color that you like and that flatters you. The best starting point for this might be in checking out your wardrobe. If you consistently choose pastels (or neutrals), then these are probably the colors that you would be most happy living with.

• Don't worry about breaking rules. The cliché about using light colors to make a room look larger and dark colors to make a room look smaller has a grain of truth in it. However, dark colors create instant warmth and drama. Your choice of color should depend less on rules than on your own emotional responses. Some people need to live with sunny colors in order to be happy; if you love bright yellow, you don't have to confine it to your kitchen. If you like it, even lavender can come out of the bedroom and into the living room.

• Don't be shy. The vibrant color that you intuitively respond to will give you far more pleasure than the dull color you think is in good taste.

The easiest color scheme starts with one dominant color plus white. Any color accented by white has a crisp, fresh look. Think of the variety this gives you: yellow and white; gray and white; blue and white; tan and white; navy and white. For a sunny-looking breakfast room, you might paint the walls a deep daisy yellow and the ceiling, woodwork, and doors a high-gloss white. If the chairs have cushions, choose a yellow-and-white pinstripe pattern or a country English pattern with a yellow background and brightly colored flowers. A botanical print on the wall will add an extra dash of color, and straw matting or a pastel rag rug will complete the look.

The safest color scheme calls for neutrals—beige and gray, primarily.

Until a few years ago, gray was one of the most underestimated colors in design. New York decorator Angelo Donghia changed that when he started painting walls a pale gray as a blend for gray flannel upholstery on the furniture. Gray is an ideal background for bright accent colors such as pink, red, yellow, and white.

Beige looks good with an enormous range of accessory colors, is pleasing to the eye over time, and can be given a very high-fashion look. When using beige in a modern room, consider a monochromatic scheme where all the shades are in the beige family. Match rugs, upholstery, and drapery fabric to the wall color. This takes the guesswork out of decorating and also creates a very serene look.

The prettiest color schemes are pastels. Colors such as sky blue and melon are a natural background for floral-patterned chintz or striped cotton slipcovers and curtains. Here you can let your imagination take over—add ruffles, trim the pillows with ribbon, use full, flouncy curtains. Anything that's soft, pretty, and decorative will look right in a pastel room.

The most dramatic color schemes involve very dark colors, such as chocolate brown, burgundy, and hunter green. Billy Baldwin, who was sometimes called the dean of American decorators, used very dark brown on the walls of his New York studio apartment and then slipcovered all his furniture in off-white linen. The look is cool and very urbane.

Consider dark colors if your walls are in poor condition. With dark paint, you can hide imperfections that would be noticeable if the walls were a lighter color.

Dark colors are often chosen by wealthy people because the deep shades serve as a good background for artwork. You don't need to be rich to adapt the principle: Your collection of drawings, posters, or prints would look terrific against a hunter green wall.

Dark colors also create a cozy, inviting atmosphere that's almost impossible to duplicate with white or pastels. Brighten the room by using light-colored upholstery on your furniture.

The most unexpected color scheme involves red. Many people steer clear of red because they are afraid that it would be difficult to live with over time. That's a misconception. A color that's popularly called Chinese red—a deep, dark red—has long been a favorite among decorators because it looks so opulent. Red becomes a neutral when it's on the wall and looks good with almost any print or upholstery color. In modern rooms, red is beautiful with toast or deep beige upholstery and fabrics; in traditional rooms, look for stripes and floral patterns in cotton, silk, or brocade.

An always-right choice is white. Although decorators tend to use color on walls, many architects still opt for white. White walls can give a room a pristine, modern look that's very restful to live with. For an extremely modern and bold look, pick a pure white that isn't tinged with cream or gray. Pure white will set off the colors of your upholstery, rugs, and artwork.

For a bit of extra style, consider painting your ceiling a pale aqua or sky blue. It's a very pretty touch in a white room.

Step Two: Buying the Paint

The best place to buy paint is at a big paint store where many manufacturers are represented. Some stores have their own unbranded paints; I tend to avoid buying them because I'm never sure whether I'm getting a bargain or being taken.

There's only one rule in buying paint: Always buy the best you can afford. The cost of paint is pegged to the amount of pigment in it; if you buy cheap paint, you'll be getting less pigment and more filler. This may mean that you'll need an extra coat so the less expensive brand would cost you more in the long run.

The paint store will give you color strips, but never make your final decision at the store. Colors look different in different lights. Bring the strips home and tape them up on the wall and look at the colors under daylight and artificial lighting. If you're debating between two shades, choose the lighter one.

If your walls are in excellent condition, you might want to try giving them a high-gloss or semigloss finish. The gloss reflects light, making any room brighter and prettier.

If you're painting the walls yourself, use a water-base paint. It's easier to clean up than an oil-base paint. Professional house painters claim that an oil-base paint gives a deeper, more lasting coverage. I don't believe them: I think that's one way of creating a mystique about their profession.

Step Three: Painting the Room

When you're doing the painting, outline the ceiling, doors, and woodwork with a brush and then paint in the walls with a roller. If you tape the edges of the woodwork first, the paint won't splatter on the wood and you will get a clean edge.

Unless you're painting over a similar color, you'll always need two coats. Before you start, do a test area to make sure that you like the color. If there's only a small amount of paint left after the job is done, pour this into an airtight bottle to use for touchups.

When you're having the walls painted by a professional, be there when the first coat is completed. If you want the color deepened or lightened, that's the time to make the decision.

Textured paints

Textured paints are "heavy" paints that automatically cover cracks, flaked paint, or damaged wallpaper. The major drawback of textured paints is that they are difficult to remove, and if you're renting, you should consult your landlord before proceeding.

There are several different types of textured paints. Some are sand-impregnated; others are smooth and become interesting by the way in which they are applied. For instance, a smooth finish would give you an adobe look if applied with a brush, but if applied with a broom, sponge, or roller, the effect would be very different. Textured paints leave a wide area for creativity.

Other Wall Treatments

Fabric

Fabric-covered walls are a beautiful alternative to painted walls, particularly if your walls are in poor condition. However, if your walls are in bad shape, you'll want to make certain that the fabric stands away from the wall. Nail a furring strip (a 1 × 2-inch strip of wood) on the top and bottom of the wall and then staple fabric to the strip. It's best to pleat fabric as you staple. Cover staples with ribbon or trim.

An elegant variation is to use curtain rods at the ceiling and baseboards. The fabric is then hemmed and gathered onto the curtain rod. This is more complicated than stapling because it calls for hemming the fabric exactly to fit onto the rods.

Egon von Furstenburg used brown paisley fabric to curtain the walls of a small dining room. He repeated the paisley on the chair cushions and in the tablecloth. The many yards of paisley gave the room a warm, intimate, and very expensive look.

Wood Paneling

While many homeowners choose paneling, few apartment dwellers make use of it on their walls. But there's no reason for apartment owners to neglect paneling. The wood comes in

4 × 8-foot sections and isn't difficult to mount or impossible to remove. There are many kinds of woods available. One of the most expensive is mahogany, and it gives a rich, established look; one of the least expensive is yellow pine, and it is light enough to be stained any shade.

Wallpaper

Wallpaper turns four walls into a memorable setting. Imagine a sunny living room with luscious cabbage roses, a kitchen with a strawberry pattern, a boy's room with tartan red plaid, and a small bathroom with a scattering of purple violets.

Wallpaper tends to be expensive, and you might want to use it only in small areas of the house, such as an entrance foyer, hallway, bathroom, or kitchen. As a rule of thumb in selecting prints, use small patterns for small areas and larger patterns for big areas such as the living room or bedroom. (For kitchens and bathrooms, use a washable vinyl paper.)

Be careful when choosing a wallpaper color for the living room. Colors seem to become brighter in bigger spaces. Save brights for foyers, bathrooms, and kitchens, where a flare of color will be welcome.

Some people are afraid of pattern—afraid that it will drive them crazy after a while. It won't. Small, overall repeat patterns tend to blend into the background and create coziness without dominating. For a super-stylish look, buy a wallpaper that has a coordinating pattern and use the smaller pattern on the ceiling.

Often there is a fabric that matches or blends with the wallpaper. Coordinating fabrics will allow you to do a whole room in variations of a pattern. If you're nervous about mixing patterns, here's a decorator maxim: Start with one largish pattern, one medium-size, and one smaller. The different scales will create a visual balance.

Sometimes wallpaper is chosen because it will add texture and a distinguished look to a room. One of the best wallpapers for this is a beige grasscloth. It gives a room background interest without calling attention to itself.

You needn't be confined to traditional wallpapers. David Hicks, a top English interior designer, covered the walls of a drawing room with brown wrapping paper. The low-key color was a perfect foil for the patterned carpeting and modern furniture in the room. Wrapping paper can be bought in rolls from stationery stores. It's not as heavy as wallpaper and takes very careful handling so it doesn't crumple.

If you're handy, you can hang wallpaper yourself. Many wallpapers now come with prepasted backs so that it's only necessary to wet the glue and apply them. In my opinion, putting up wallpaper is a two-person job—and a job for two very patient people at that. But it can be done, and it might be worth considering. I would suggest that you choose a pattern that doesn't have to be perfectly matched. Stay away from plaids and horizontal patterns.

Don't wallpaper any walls that are less than perfect. Rather than covering the cracks or imperfections, wallpaper seems to emphasize them.

If you're a rental tenant, consider buying a "strippable" wallpaper. This will help you avoid the cost of having the wallpaper removed when you move.

Mirrors

For sparkle and elegance, almost no decorative accent can duplicate the power of mirrors. Whether it's a small framed tabletop mirror or a completely mirrored wall, the effect is always powerful.

A mirrored wall will double the size of your room visually. Many people worry that they'll feel self-conscious with a mirrored wall—and yet one rarely does. If you're a rental tenant, then mirrors should be mounted on removable panels.

You can have the look of mirroring without the cost by using mirrored squares. The squares are usually about $1 for a 12 × 12-inch self-adhesive tile. Mirror squares can be cut with a small knife which is sold at most paint and hardware stores. Be sure to mark the wall in advance so the squares are installed on a perfect horizontal and vertical line. This can be done by using a plumb line: Tack a chalked string to the ceiling and weight the string with a pair of scissors so it will hang absolutely straight. The chalk of the string will lightly mark the wall.

Look for ways to use mirroring:

• Mirror the bathroom ceiling. Although some people use

mirror squares for this, I believe that mirrored ceilings should be installed by an expert. Since it's a small area, it's not a particularly expensive installation.

• Hang a mirror over the sofa. Precut rectangles in sizes up to 5 feet are widely available and usually cost less than $100. Use a large round mirror over a buffet in the dining room.

• Brass-framed closet mirrors from the dime store make a handsome statement when five or six are hung side by side in the living room. (See page 117.)

• If you're fortunate enough to have deeply set windows, mirror the reveals. The mirroring will frame the windows and reflect the street scenes from different angles, depending on where you're standing in the room. (See page 121.)

• Mirror the platform of a built-in bed to make it "float."

• Instead of buying an étagère, mirror a small wall and install glass shelves. Use the shelves for a mixture of books and mementos. Leave enough empty space so that the mirror reflects the objects and the room.

Artwork

Even people who are sure about their taste sometimes become hesitant over their choice of artwork. The rule here is that there are no rules. There is no such thing as correct taste in painting or artwork—one critic's passion is another's poison.

• Artwork should add something to your room. It should either add color, add design interest, or be so personal that it adds a dimesion to your life. The best example of that is photographs. Most people keep pictures tucked away. That's a shame. Wouldn't it be nice to have a long table with all your favorite pictures framed so that you could see them every day? Or a corkboard wall with the pictures thumbtacked on? We need our personal lives around us.

• One of my favorite apartments belongs to the photographer Richard Steedman. He travels the world shooting for top magazines, and wherever he goes, he buys crafts. His taste is very eclectic: a beaded necklace from Africa, a kilim from Turkey, and a Mexican tapestry are hung side by side on the wall with a handsome collection of early American trade signs. A decorator might say that the apartment is overcrowded and that any one of the pieces is strong enough to serve as a focal point. But everyone who comes into the apartment loves the assortment and feels instantly at home. The lesson here (if there is one) is to hang everything around you that you love.

• Kodak has developed a process which allows one to enlarge pictures to almost any size. It's possible to have a poster-size mural from a small snapshot or a postcard. Alan Buchsbaum blew up a picture of a rose with a drop of dew on it to an 8-foot size for his SoHo loft; another friend had four pictures of the Eiffel Tower, each taken at a different time of the day, blown up and placed side by side in his small apartment.

• Almost any collection can be displayed in an interesting way. I once saw a collection of old tin cookie forms in a Chicago kitchen. It looked terrific. A fisherman hung his fishing rods over the couch of his New York apartment and they looked like three-dimensional art.

• A little humor can go a long way with artwork. Designer Robert Hart hung a small, ornately carved antique picture frame over a Shaker dresser with nothing inside the frame.

• The Shakers hung chairs and work objects, such as brooms and farm implements, on the wall. Some architects have updated this approach by hanging bright-red steel folding chairs. A friend hangs his yellow bicycle from heavy hooks in his hallway. It looks very good.

• Many of the ethnic rugs make beautiful wall hangings. The shop at the United Nations always has a lovely selection of small, very pretty handwoven kilims in bright colors; so do many of the Indian and Far Eastern import shops. To hang a rug, nail a 1 × 2-inch wood strip to the wall and tack the rug to it.

• Handmade quilts make beautiful wall hangings. They don't have to be antique or precious but they should be special.

• A friend is a Paul Newman buff. She's been cutting out pictures and stories about him for as long as I can remember. She recently glued them to the kitchen wall, montage-style. It's wonderful to see those blue eyes repeated over and over again.

Flooring

Carpeting and Rugs

Although the starting point of a decorating project is the walls and the color scheme, many people forget that floors are a major element of every home or apartment—and they give them scant attention.

Carpeting is the easiest way to give an apartment or home a finished look—particularly when the carpeting matches the walls. This is especially effective in small rooms, in which a scattering of rugs might produce a cluttered and "busy" effect.

Gray industrial carpeting was the big look of the '70s and will probably always remain popular with those whose taste is architectural. Industrial carpeting is not cheap. But it wears well, looks sophisticated, and is an excellent foil to white walls, leather furniture, and chrome or glass coffee tables. It works particularly well in rooms in which platforms are used, because the flat finish allows it to follow the form of the strip beneath it.

Rugs are decorative accessories as well as floor coverings. Like any decoration, they reflect your personal taste, and they add an interesting and colorful touch to a room.

Traditional oriental rugs are like magic—they seem to fit in perfectly with any style of furniture. In an ultramodern room, they soften the hard edges; in a traditional room, they blend in comfortably.

Two of the most stylish looks in rugs are actually the least expensive:

• Old-fashioned rag rugs are being woven now in a pastel palette. A sky blue, pale pink, and sunshine yellow rug is a marvelous color accent in rooms with light-colored walls or casual furniture, such as wicker or country pine. Another advantage is that rag rugs are washable.

• Dhurries are the traditional flat-weave rugs from India and Pakistan. The designs and colors are sensational—pastel geometric patterns against a natural beige background. If you have trouble imagining how pretty this can be, ask to see dhurries at most department stores. You'll be amazed by the prices (an 8 × 11 rug is often less than $500) and by their beauty.

Pickled and Painted Floors

My own favorite floor treatments are either "pickled" floors or floors that have been covered with deck paint.

To pickle a floor, strip it raw and then varnish with at least three layers of very thin stain before a polyurethane sealer is applied. The stain allows the grain of the floor to show through. This is generally an expensive process when outside contractors do it, because time has to be allowed for the floors to dry between applications. You can cut costs by having floors professionally sanded and then doing the staining yourself. Plan to spend at least a week on the job—but you'll have a showpiece in return for your time.

Deck paint is one of the great inventions. You can easily paint the floor with a roller, and the deck paint is durable and available in a wide range of colors. I once saw a beautiful penthouse apartment where the walls were white, the ceiling was sky blue, and the floors were painted white. It was furnished with inexpensive wicker and with sisal rugs, and there were white geraniums in the windows. The white floor gave the apartment its "look."

With either pickled or painted floors, you can go one step

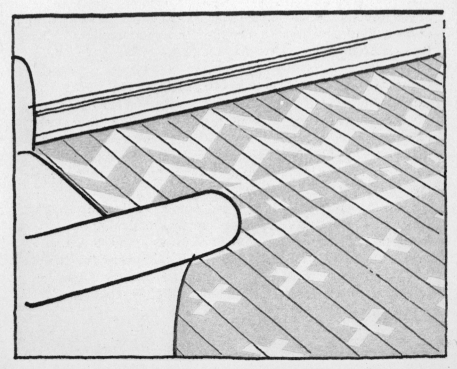

further by painting or stenciling a border around the room. Stencil kits are available at most paint stores, and they are easy to work with. You don't have to be an artist to do a stenciled floor; you simply have to be patient enough to tape the stencil down and paint in the cutouts.

Gloria Vanderbilt designed a patchwork bedroom for herself which was envied even by those people who already have everything. She covered the walls and floor in a matching quilt-patterned patchwork. The floors were a montage of fabrics, each piece separately cut and glued. To protect the fabric, the floors were heavily coated with polyurethane. (See page 101.)

To create a two-toned geometric pattern with deck paint: Paint the first color on the floor, using a roller. Allow it to dry thoroughly. Use paint-resistant masking tape to outline the geometric pattern. Paint your geometric pattern over the first coat with the contrasting color; when it's dry, apply a second coat. Peel the tape off.

The painted floor shown in the illustration was stenciled with a pattern that's available at most paint stores. Stenciling a floor isn't difficult, but it does call for patience. Tape the stencil to the floor and paint in the precut pattern. Stenciling kits with directions are available for less than $10.

Linoleum Tiles

Linoleum tiles are always an interesting choice of flooring. They've recently become more popular as manufacturers have introduced finishes and colors that are designed for living rooms rather than kitchens. Tiles can be cut by hand, and many have prepasted backs, which makes installation easy. The secret in using linoleum tiles stylishly is in being bold with your choice of pattern. Use a border or mix in two or three colors. Here are some pattern ideas. Patterned linoleum flooring looks best when you use pure colors instead of marbleized ones.

Window Coverings

Window treatments are the finishing touch in a decorating scheme. Your choice of window covering will depend on whether you are working with high apartment windows or traditional casement windows.

In high-rise apartments, window treatments are more of a challenge because there are more problems: The long stretch of windows are boring and cold; the air-conditioning and heating units often mar the window wall; and the view which these windows were meant to frame is often the less-than-glorious vision of your neighbor across the street.

The ideal solution is vertical blinds. They allow light to come in but enable you to have complete privacy. If verticals are hung ceiling to floor about a foot in front of windows, they will cover the radiator and air conditioner and also allow you an inconspicuous place for stereo speakers.

Vertical shades are available in a full palette of colors, and it is easy to find a color that matches or blends with your wall.

The updated version of old-fashioned venetian blinds—the narrow-slatted steel blinds—is a very crisp, fashionable window coverng in high rises. Again, these blinds are available in a wide range of colors, and it's easy to find a ready-made size for apartment windows.

In traditional rooms that have pretty windows and a nice view, you'll want to call attention to the windows. Thus, your window treatment should be showy and as decorative as the walls and upholstery.

Curtains and drapes are always an appropriate choice in a traditional room. I believe curtains should always be custom-made, using a fabric that works with your upholstery and wall color. It's easy to make draperies or curtains yourself. Notions shops carry "drapery tape" which is sewn to the top of the fabric and creates pockets for the drapery hooks. An offbeat choice of curtain fabric is natural muslin, which sells for less than $1 per yard and looks wonderful when it's gathered very fully on a curtain rod. The muslin is light enough to billow in the breeze, and it has a most graceful drape.

Shutters always look crisp, fresh, and "right" in casement

windows. Paint shutters white or stain them to match the woodwork. Louvered doors are a less expensive alternative to shutters. (Shutter slats open and close; louvered door slats are in a fixed position.) The look is similar; compare prices. If possible, spray paint louvers or shutters before they are installed. It's very time-consuming to paint them by hand.

• In order to give the impression of a higher ceiling, and thus a more spacious proportioning of the room, always hang draperies and curtains from the top of the wall rather than at the top of the window.

Lighting

There are fads in lighting just as there are in fashion. For years, track lighting was considered *de rigueur* by decorators. Generally, though, track lights are an expense without a cause: The tracks tend to be costly; the spotlights are four or five times as expensive as ordinary light bulbs, and many more spots are required to light a room than when using ordinary table lamps.

The best time to use tracks is when you want to spotlight a picture or use overhead lights as "grow lights" for plants.

• A Hollywood beauty trick: use pink light bulbs in the bedroom. It's the most flattering color for a woman's skin and literally creates a soft, rosy glow in a room.

• I love lighting that is adapted from other fields. One of my favorites is the photographer's lamp, which is, essentially, a pole lamp with a light that's protected by a white silky-looking umbrella. Photographers use this as soft lighting for beauty shots, and it is a very flattering glow.

Such umbrellas can be clipped onto any pole; they are available at photography supply stores. A 28-inch-wide umbrella costs about $11; a 42-inch-wide umbrella costs about $15; and the clip costs about $7.

Chapter Two
Under $25

Here is a decorating truism: Almost anything looks prettier with a border. Think about this for a minute and you'll realize how often you have seen ordinary pillows, draperies, and slipcovers transformed into beautiful showpieces by being trimmed with ribbons, sequins, or tassels. Notions shops are the places to buy these trims, but first start looking for inspiration in expensive stores that specialize in custom work. There you'll see how a ribbon border and a few sequins scattered across a floral-patterned pillow doubles the price; the same is true of draperies. Most of the top traditional decorators trim curtains with ribbons and give upholstery added richness with braided edges.

Let the sun shine in: Use your windows as a decorative focal point without blocking the view by applying stencils to panes of glass.

How-to: Stencils are widely availabe in paint stores and craft shops. Tape the stencil to the window and paint inside the cut-out area. The best color to use is white—it has a nice frosty clean look.

Most frames that look great cost a fortune. But for an inexpensive, museum-quality picture frame, try this: Screw mirror clamps into place and slide glass cut to size and a mat cut to size into the clamps; the top clamps are dropped into place (not screwed in) so that it's easy to remove glass, matting, or picture. The flat-to-the-wall, unframed, clean-cut edges give it a pristine quality. Buy glass and have it cut at a glass/mirror shop.

Frame your pictures handsomely: Instead of using the plain mat that comes with a standard picture frame, cover that mat with patterned wrapping paper or fabric. Use patterned mats when hanging a grouping of pictures. The mats will pull together disparate subjects and give a unified look to any arrangement of artwork.

How-to: Buy frames and cardboard mats from a dimestore. When cutting patterned fabric or paper, allow at least one inch all around. Wrap the overlap to the back of the mat and glue. As a finishing touch, paint the frames to match the pattern of the mat. The frames shown in the illustration were painted cherry red.

One of the most amusing new products at paint stores is "black-board paint." It allows you to give your child his own private gallery. The paint is about $7 per pint and is available in slate black and "schoolboard" green. You might also want to give yourself a blackboard wall in the kitchen or sewing room. Jot down your favorite recipes or notes to yourself. Blackboard walls by the telephone are terrific for doodlers!

Add extra storage without taking up precious wall space by building a high shelf. You can use this idea in the kitchen to store cookbooks, in the living room to show off a collection, and in the den to keep the papers and books you don't use regularly.

How-to: Use ¾-inch clear pine for the shelf and L-shaped shelf brackets as supports. The long part of the brackets should be against the wall; screw bracket into a butterfly hinge for additional support. Place brackets closer together if shelf will be supporting heavy objects.

Transform an old chest of drawers into a combination dresser/ headboard. This arrangement is especially suited to studio apartments and to small bedrooms, where space is limited and every inch must be put to use. If you already own an old chest of drawers, the only money you will have to spend is a few dollars for a fresh coat of paint.

How-to: If you're painting the back of the chest, be sure to sand it smooth. Either paint it a color that will match or contrast with your linens. Another approach: staple fabric or matching sheeting to the back. After stapling it around all four sides, edge it with binding tape or ribbon.

Have fun with children's furniture by painting faces on an old chest of drawers. When you use the knob of a drawer for a nose, you have a natural starting point for the rest of the face. Give yourself confidence by first practicing with pencil and paper.

How-to: Turn the chest on its back so that you are painting on a horizontal surface. Otherwise, the paint may dribble down. Draw the outline in pencil first, then trace over it with a fine-line brush.

Kids respond to bright colors. If you want to add cheer to a child's room, try painting an old chest of drawers so that each drawer is a different color. The finished product may not be a candidate for a museum, but your child will love it.

How-to: For children's furniture, always use high-gloss paint, because it leaves a surface that washes easily.

For a homey touch, add a colonial-style shelf over the window and use it to show off plants and art objects. One of the best places to find this type of shelf is at unpainted furniture stores. Either paint the shelf to match the wall or stain it to match the window frames or furniture.

Important: Before you buy unpainted furniture, compare prices on similar pieces of finished furniture. There are some very good buys in unfinished furniture, but you have to pick and choose very carefully. Many of the pieces are poorly proportioned and not very interesting. One way to give unfinished furniture a more expensive look is by replacing ordinary knobs with the porcelain or plastic knobs available at many house-wares stores.

How-to: Most precut shelving units come with their own hardware or have a cutout at the back that allows the bracket to slide onto a nail or screw in the wall. Stain the brackets and shelves before they are installed—it's easier that way! Stain is available in many different types of finish, from mahogany to pine color. Follow the directions on the can, and remember, the crucial difference between a beautifully stained piece and an amateur job is in having the patience to sand lightly between a first and second application. (Hint: Apply with soft cloth as a brush can leave marks.)

A shelf behind the sofa creates a striking focal point for a room. The shelf gives you an ideal place for a reading lamp and a show-off area for art objects. For a built-in look, paint the shelf with high-gloss enamel to match the wall color. Install the shelf with brackets.

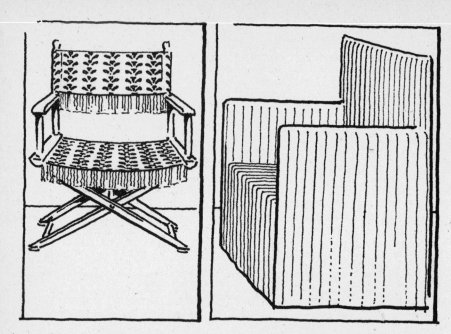

A bit of imagination goes a long way. In the illustration shown here, an inexpensive director's chair has been covered with a cheerful print that was sewn over the canvas cover. For extra style, add an edging of braid or tassels.

On the right, an old chair destined for the dump was given a second life with a bright striped chintz cover.

How-to: The no-guesswork way to make slipcovers is to pin the pieces together on the chair, working with the wrong side of the fabric. Seam the fabric after you're sure that it's a perfect fit.

Fans glamorize walls. The inexpensive paper fans at oriental import shops take on added allure when several are hung against a dark-colored wall.

How-to: Determine in advance how far apart you want the fans to be. For example, if you are covering a space 6 feet wide and are using three fans, then the bottom of the fans might be mounted at 2-foot intervals for the best effect. Mark the wall lightly with a pencil and tack through the bottom of each fan with a very thin nail.

Important: When mounting a delicate object over a seating area, be sure to hang it high enough so it isn't touched when one sits back.

Next to raising the roof, the best way to give your room the look of a higher ceiling is by using low furniture and built-in platforms. Here, an additional sleight-of-hand was used: a wavy design painted low on a wall leaves a long expanse of wall above it, so that the ceiling appears to be higher.

How-to: To make the wavy lines, start by penciling in squares the width and height of the design. Then draw the lower part of the wave, starting at the bottom of each box and rising at the center of that box, etc. To paint in the design, outline each color with a narrow brush and then fill it in with a wider brush. Although you can use any colors, a very effective scheme is to use three shades of the same color. You can mix the shades yourself: Choose the darkest color and then temper it with white for the next two areas.

A Japanese umbrella makes a very pretty lighting fixture in any room of your house. The lacquered paper softens the light into a subtle glow. In small rooms, hang it close to the ceiling; in larger spaces, allow it to drop so light will also reflect off the ceiling. Japanese umbrellas come in a wide variety of sizes. Small ones are attractive in hallways and entrance foyers.

How-to: Open the umbrella and then saw the handle. Tie cord or thin wire to three spokes of the umbrella. Wrap the wire around the old lighting fixture or thumbtack it to your ceiling.

Have you ever wished you could have an extra closet without building one? Here's an ideal solution: Drape a table with fabric or a tapestry and hang café curtains in the front section. Install a rod or dowel underneath the table for hanging blouses or pants.

How-to: To make your extra closet, have a dowel cut to size at the lumberyard. A dowel is a round of wood that looks like a broom handle. Install the dowel on half-round brass brackets from the hardware store.

A stylish, easy-to-store service table for parties or company dinners is the wallpaper hanger's table. The legs fold compactly, and the table top is removable.

How-to: The "legs" for your table cost about $35, and are available at most paint stores. To make the table, first decide how high you want it to be by moving the "legs" up and down. When you find your desired height, saw off the extra extension of wood (see illustration). For your tabletop, use a piece of plywood at least ½-inch thick. You can stain and varnish the top to give it a more finished look.

A "wall necklace" of test tubes (originally designed by Eric Broaddus) can be hung on your wall to give an arty, modern look. The tubes are held together by copper wire attached to hooks in the wall and twisted around the top and bottom of the tubes. Test tubes are available through medical supply stores and cost from 25¢ to 75¢, depending on size.

Create an edible centerpiece. A pear becomes an unexpected vase for flowers in an arrangement designed by New York florist Ronaldo Maia (see illustration). Using any firm fleshed fruit or vegetable (e.g., acorn squash, pumpkin), hollow out a narrow area for a glass medical test tube and push it into the fruit gently. The test tube costs less than 50¢ and is available at medical supply stores.

Before you run out and buy posters to cover up blank walls, consider this eye-catching alternative: Japanese fans bunched together become the focal point of a room. They're lightweight and easy to work with. Either tack them to the wall or use two-sided tape. Oriental import shops offer the best variety of paper fans.

The oversized paper lantern has become an interior design classic. The key to giving the lantern a classy look is in buying it one size bigger than you think you need. The lanterns are available in oriental import shops, and most sizes cost less than $15.

Any picture looks prettier when it's beautifully hung. Illustrated here are wide ribbons tied with big, floppy bows. They make inexpensive pictures look luxurious and regal.

How-to: Hang the picture with picture wire and cover the wire with the ribbon.

You can make an unusual low table with wine bottles that's dramatic—and inexpensive. The wine bottles provide an unusual base, and a board provides the top surface.

How-to: You will need a drill or keyhole saw to create the openings for the bottle necks. The best bottles to use are champagne magnums, which you can usually get from an accommodating restaurateur. (Unfortunately, he will probably not give you the ones full of champagne!) Fill bottles with water or sand for additional stability.

Build an attractive yarn holder to keep next to your favorite chair in the house.

How-to: You will need a keyhole saw for this project. Take two squares of wood, gently rounded at the edges, and drill holes as shown in the illustration. Now stitch a piece of canvas over two dowels. Insert these two dowels in the top two holes of the yarn holder. Place a third dowel in the lower hole for support.

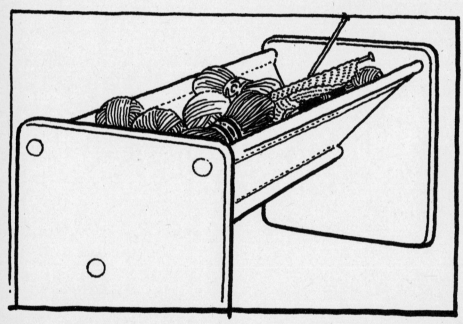

No place to put magazines and newspapers? A clothes drying rack is an ideal solution to your problem. Racks are available at houseware shops.

Give ordinary wood bookshelves a custom-built look with molding. Most lumberyards carry a wide variety of embossed molding that costs less than 50¢ per foot.

How-to: Buy a molding that is the same width and length as your bookshelf (or have it cut to size at the lumberyard). Use thin nails to mount. Stain the molding to match the shelf.

You can get the look of stenciled or handpainted walls with ordinary rubber stamps. Yes, the kind of stamps that are used in offices can be used in your home to create gaily patterned walls almost instantly.

How-to: First of all, consider the type of pattern you would like on your wall. A flower? A leaf? Draw your own pattern, or trace one from a magazine or wallpaper book. Next, go to an office supply shop and have the outlines of your pattern duplicated on a stamp. Inks are available in many colors.

An ordinary dresser takes on a 19th century look when it's glamorized with pre-split bamboo. For an authentic looking finish, paint the furniture black and add brass knobs.

How-to: You can either find split bamboo by checking under "Bamboo" in the Yellow Pages or by buying a small split bamboo window shade from an oriental shop and using the slats. Cut the edges on the diagonal so the corners will match (see illustration). Draw a pencil outline of where the bamboo will be placed and then turn the chest on its back and, using a white glue that doesn't dry quickly, move the bamboo around until it's perfectly placed. Carefully match the edges. Let the glue dry thoroughly before you stand the chest up again.

Add a touch of whimsy to your bedroom with a colorful hand-painted mural. This oversized cloud-shaped cartoon is easy enough for any amateur to paint.

How-to: First draw in the outline of the cloud with a pencil. Then, using regular wall paints, outline the drawing with a fine brush and fill in with a wider brush. A graphic of this sort is more of an act of courage than an artistic achievement, so don't worry if your lines aren't perfectly straight. Choose your colors boldly: In a yellow room, you might want a bright red cloud; or in a white room, you might want a royal blue cloud.

Ordinary white Styrofoam cups become the material for a wall sculpture. With a dab of glue, the cups hold instantly to the wall. The finished look is as beautiful as any artists' three-dimensional sculpture and the cost is less than $5. But be fore-warned: Lining up the cups takes time and patience. You'll have to draw diagonal pencil or chalk lines on the wall as guide-lines for the pattern. Don't glue up your first cup until you're sure that all the lines are straight and measured correctly.

Time is money, and nothing gives that adage more truth than stenciled walls. It would cost a fortune to buy and install wallpaper like this—but the materials for stenciling cost only a few dollars. The finished effect of a completely stenciled wall is breathtakingly beautiful.

How-to: Stencils are widely available at paint stores and crafts shops. Just tape them onto the wall, then paint inside the cutouts, using regular wall paint. Is it difficult? Absolutely not. It's more like a labor of love, and each completed pattern is a special source of pride for you.

Sometimes the homeliest objects take on a totally new look because of the way in which they are displayed. The orange crates in the illustration, for instance, are the focal point of a young architect's apartment. Hung at the right distance from each other and filled with books and a pleasant collection of art objects, they become valuable additions to the room.

How-to: All the crates must be exactly the same size and in very good condition. Keep looking until you find a "matched set." To hang: either screw them into the wall using "molly bolts" or use heavy duty picture hangers. Picture hangers are designed to hold weights up to several hundred pounds; buy hangers that are at least triple the weight that you think you'll need. Use one on either side of each box and a center one for balance.

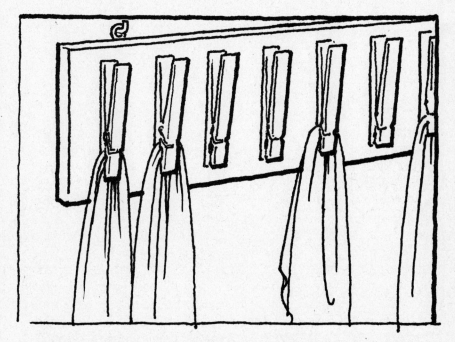

A plywood board with clothespins glued to it has casual chic for a kitchen or bathroom. Paint the board a bright color and use clothespins of a contrasting color.

The handmade quilts you own should be shown off as a work of art. To hang it: first attach a thin strip of wood to the wall at the proper height. Use small nails to tack the quilt to the wood.

The plainest table takes on a new look with a centerpiece. A single flower can be as decorative as an expensive bouquet when it's dramatically displayed. My favorite setting is a small glass bowl with a little water and black pebbles on the bottom to support the stem. Black pebbles are available at florist shops. For variety, use seashells, rocks, or clear marbles.

For either a window that gets too much sun or one that doesn't get enough: Hang a picture in front of the window. Attach with long wires at the top of the window frame.

Many decorators collect bottles—Perrier bottles, wine and champagne bottles, instant-coffee containers, and even mustard jars—to use for flower arrangements. The prettiest arrangements use a mixture of four or five different-size bottles, each bottle with a different type of flower. Casual mismatching has an offbeat chic that's hard to beat.

Another flower fad: using chemical beakers or flasks for flowers. This started a couple of years ago when the beakers began selling in department stores and decorator shops. Prices are about double the amount one would pay at a medical supply house. Many of these beakers are gracefully shaped with long necks that are perfect for a single flower.

When you're using a clear glass flower container, you might want to add a drop of colored food dye to the water.

Rhonda Racz, a New York publicist with a charming blue-and-white country-style apartment, uses antique cut-crystal vinegar and oil containers to hold daisies. Other elegant flower holders: old perfume bottles, antique liquor decanters, or old ceramic pitchers.

How would you like to have wall-to-wall carpeting for practically nothing? You can make a stunning one-of-a-kind patchwork carpet with sample squares. Many carpeting shops have small samples which they will give to customers for free. Or try buying remnants for a nominal amount. When these pieces are put together on the floor, the variation in color and texture can be much more interesting than the most expensive carpet.

How-to: Shop for squares at least 1 foot square until you have enough in one color grouping to give your carpeting a unified look. The colors don't have to match, but they should blend nicely together. Spread the squares on the floor and work with them until you're satisfied with the pattern. Install the squares on the floor with heavy-duty tape that is sticky on both sides. It's called carpeting tape, and hardware stores carry it.

●

Transform a drab kitchen into a cheery personal place with a complete wall montage of pictures that have personal meaning to you. This is a way of creating your own "wallpaper," and there are limitless possibilities. Cut pictures out of magazines; use photographs of family and friends; use travel postcards. Wine enthusiasts create beautiful walls by using colorful labels from their favorite bottles, and movie buffs save up pictures from fan magazines.

How-to: You can line up the pictures in an orderly fashion, or be more creative and mix big pictures and small pictures. Or create an abstract by cutting out parts of the pictures, such as eyes and mouths. After you've glued the pictures up, coat the wall with polyurethane so the pictures won't discolor.

●

Your kitchen windowsill can be a decorative focal point if you buy a wood or metal planter box and plant it full of herbs or flowers. One of the prettiest looks for May through November: a window box full of red geraniums. Or grow an herb garden to give your kitchen a fresh smell. When you're using the 7-inch-deep standard window boxes, be sure to put rocks in the bottom for drainage.

Chapter Three
Under $50

For an inexpensive seating arrangement, bring outdoor furniture inside. Stitch another fabric over the canvas slings to coordinate the chairs with the rest of your furniture.

Your dining room table will take on a dramatic new look when ordinary clay pots are used as lighting fixtures. In addition to providing a pleasing earthy texture, the pots will cast a rich, warm light on your room.

How-to: Thread wire and chain through the hole in the bottom of the pot and attach it to your light socket. The wire can be attached to a hook or outlet in the ceiling. The materials you will need to hang your pots are available at a local hardware store, but you will need knowledge of wiring before attempting this project.

Sawhorse tables are sturdy and functional, and have a sort of inverse chic in well-decorated rooms. Buy the sawhorses from a lumberyard. Use a door as a top or update the look with a slab of marble or bronze glass.

An unusual bookcase: build a pyramid-shaped étagère. It's a step up in style from regular bookshelves and an ideal way to fill out the long wall of a den or dining room.

How-to: Cut shelves in an even progression, as shown. Nail front beams the same distance in from the edge of each shelf (front and back). In the back, you'll need crossbeams for sturdiness. Nail first crossbeam from left side of lowest shelf to right side of top shelf. Use small blocks of wood the width of the crossbeam to reinforce the connection between crossbeam and shelf.

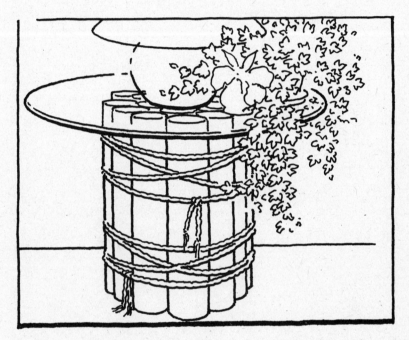

Packing tubes become a handsome table base when they are tied together with a length of drapery cord. Tubes are available at art supply stores for less than $2 each. For extra impact, lacquer the tubes dark green, midnight blue, or Chinese red. Top the tubes with a ½-inch-thick ready-made glass top.

A pop art version of the packing tube table base can be made by gluing beer or cola cans together and building them up to whatever height you choose. Use a sheet of plywood—cut in the shape of a square or circle—for the tabletop. The plywood can be painted a bright, glossy color or left natural and varnished. For this type of table, do not use a glass top, which would be too heavy for the aluminum cans to support.

Tabletop mirrors create sparkle and an infinity of images when they are angled together. Dome-topped mirrors (see illustration) are available at most dime stores for less than $12 each. To hold mirrors together, glue hinges to mirror backs.

A handpainted canvas drop cloth transforms an old chair into a work of art. Buy a lightweight canvas drop cloth at a paint supply store. Before you paint: drape cloth on chair and cut, allowing 2 inches extra for hem. Make small buttonholes in the fabric and sew buttons onto the chair beneath the cushions to keep drop cloth permanently in place. Do this before you paint the fabric. If the dropcloth doesn't fall evenly, cut it while it is on the chair, allowing 2 inches extra for a hem.

How-to: Unless you're an artist, the simplest patterns are best. Try diagonal stripes, checks, or spatters, or use a stencil cutout for a repeat pattern. Mark in your pattern with a pencil and then paint over it with a brush. A 3-inch border will give your slipcover a very professional look.

To paint on canvas: Use acrylic paints that are thinned 10% to 25% with water. Each acrylic is a bit different, and you should experiment before starting by thinning a test amount and painting it on the fabric. Allow the paint to dry thoroughly, then bend the fabric. If it cracks, you need to use more water.

•

Decorators often use canvas- or fabric-covered shutters instead of traditional wood-slat shutters as a way of adding charm and warmth to a room.

How-to: Either buy four stretched canvases made to size at an art supply store (two for the top of the window and two for below) or just buy the stretchers (frames) and cover them yourself with canvas or patterned fabric. Wrap the fabric around the stretchers and staple it to the back of the frame. The canvas or fabric allows light to come in but provides complete privacy.

•

You can have an authentic work of art for less than $40. A canvas rug, handpainted to look like the fabric rugs made by colonists in the seventeenth century, will add charm to any room.

How-to: Go to a paint store and purchase a heavy-duty drop cloth. A 5 × 8-foot size costs less than $23. Buy acrylic paints from an art supply shop. But before you begin to paint, you will need to create a pattern. The easiest patterns to execute are geometrics with a border print. With a ruler and pencil, draw in the outlines of your pattern. The border trim on the rug in the illustration looks fancy, but it's actually just a wavy line with small dabs of paint that were stenciled on. Incidentally, you can make your own cardboard stencil for this. Use a shirtboard from the laundry and do the cutout with a single-edge razor blade. When the paint is dry, apply three coats of polyurethane to protect the painted surface.

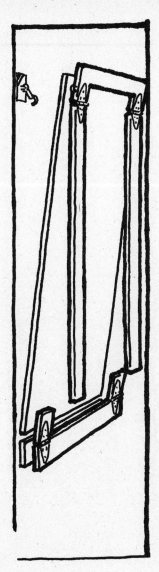

Always dreamed of being able to eat in your kitchen but cramped for space? Here's the solution: a table that folds up to the wall when not in use. And here's a nice surprise—the table doubles as a framed picture when not in use.

How-to: Purchase a rectangular board, two pieces of wood to use as the table's legs, one piece of wood to use in attaching the legs to the table's top, one piece of wood to use in attaching the table to the wall, and a final piece of wood to be used as a base on the wall. See illustration for placement of screws and hinges. When table is in place on the wall, glue a favorite poster to the table's bottom.

Convex mirrors—known as "detection mirrors"—were designed for stores as a way of spotting shoplifters, but they turn out to be a witty wall hanging. An 18-inch convex mirror is $47. Most mirror shops sell them.

How-to: Convex mirrors are lightweight and easy to hang. Most have a small lip on the back that latches onto a screw in the wall.

Don't throw away a perfectly good piece of furniture because the surface is scratched or split. Whether it's a scarred tabletop or a chest that has seen better days, you can give your furniture a facelift by adding a charming finish made with fabric or scarves.

How-to: Sand and clean the top surface thoroughly. Apply a glue that's recommended for fabrics on the wood and spread the scarf or fabric evenly across, being sure there are no air bubbles. Allow to dry and then trim evenly with a razor. Apply two coats of clear polyurethane.

Bicycle baskets make terrific yarn holders and book holders and serve as a place for all the paraphernalia that tends to litter living rooms, kids' bedrooms, and kitchens.

How-to: For attaching baskets to a table or wooden surface, use nails with wide heads. Baskets can also be hung from small cup hooks on a wall (see illustration). This allows them to tilt forward.

If you live in a modern apartment but dream of owning one of those old mansions with lots of interesting trim and molding, don't despair. You can achieve a million-dollar look with about $20 worth of molding—if you are handy or know of a good carpenter. The trick is to attach the molding so that it looks as if it's mansion-quality, and the way to do this is by mitering the corners so the edges of the molding match exactly. The molding itself is lightweight and can easily be installed with small nails.

Important: Molding should be painted with a high-gloss enamel. For the best effect, paint the molding a darker shade of the color on your walls, or pick a bright contrasting color. Finally, unless you're planning on painting your walls, be sure to paint the molding before it's installed.

More dash than cash: The elegantly finished Empire-style walls shown in the illustration are actually gracefully swagged $1-per-yard muslin gathered with big blue grosgrain bows. The bows are hooked to nails in the walls. Although it's a luxurious look, the natural color of the muslin is very low-key and easy to live with.

A classic drapery swag is an ideal window treatment for a room with a view. Choose your material according to the style of your furnishings. In a very traditional room, consider brocade or heavy silk; in a sunroom, you might want a bright chintz or a floral print.

How-to: The easiest way to create a swag is by using three separate pieces that are pleated and then stapled to a piece of wood. You'll have to experiment with the shape on a rag so that the side and center pieces have the proper contour for your window.

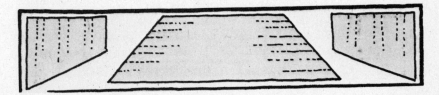

In a child's room, a collection of kites is colorful and decorative. Many of the kites are works of art and fascinating in terms of design and construction. It's an inexpensive way to be whimsical.

Use artwork to make a smallish low-ceilinged room seem larger and airier. Hang pictures about 4 inches lower than the standard eye level. This trick works best when the furniture is away from the wall and you aren't visually measuring the picture placement against a sofa or a table. In small rooms, it's always wise to scale down furnishings. Thus, a love seat might be better than a sofa and a small picture might be a wiser investment than a large one. The general rule here is that the less space you use up, the more you have left over!

A vertical herb garden is aromatic decorating at its cheeriest. Shop around for standards or plant holders that are small enough not to crowd your window.

Some things are too pretty to keep hidden away in the closet. For this one-of-a-kind window covering, you have to be lucky enough to find a beautiful piano shawl or an oversized scarf.

Lace is coming back into fashion in clothes and in decorating. The reason is the same in both areas: Lace adds a delicate, individual touch that's always romantic and pretty. In decorating, the best buy in lace is tablecloths. You can often find an 84-inch size that sells for less than $50 to use as curtains in the living room or bedroom. Other uses for lace tablecloths: as a top covering, over a comforter on the bed or as a sexy see-through shower curtain in the bathroom. (Use a plastic underliner beneath the lace.)

A plain round table becomes a confection when a contrasting top cloth is swagged and held in place with ribbon bows. To get the perfect swag: Put the top cloth on the table and safety-pin it in place before sewing.

Instead of the typical brass chain, hang lighting fixtures from curly wire. The wire is available at most housewares stores in a wide variety of colors. To keep the curl, thread heavy-duty transparent fishing line through cord to bear fixture weight.

Important: It's easy to wire a chandelier-style hanging lamp. The components are at the hardware store: socket, lamp wire (available in black and white and sold by the foot), and a plug. The wire is attached to the socket on one end and the plug on the other. If you've never made such connections, then ask the hardware salesman to show you how; it's easy. Once you know how to wire a lamp, you'll have lots of ideas for making lamps out of materials that are around the house.

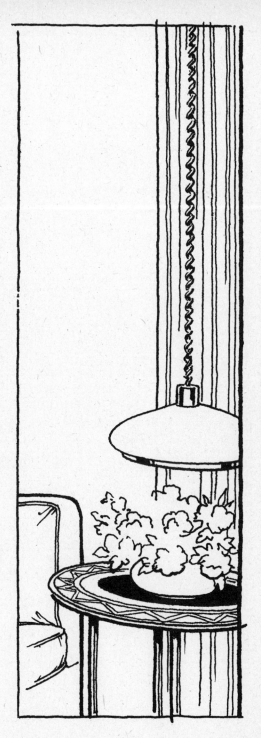

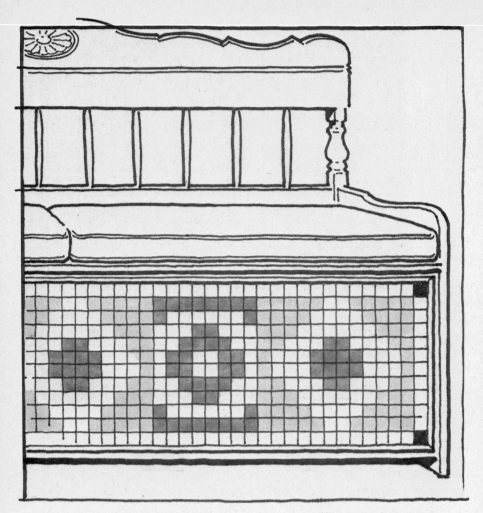

Tiny tiles used to be a nightmare to install, but now they're the easiest of all tile installations, because they come on net backings. Cut your pattern through the net and then apply the net-backed tiles to any surface with slow-drying glue. In the illustration, the tiles have been placed on the front panel of a storage bench.

Turn an ordinary poster or picture into an extraordinary graphic. The parts become more interesting than the whole when they are sectioned off.

How-to: Glue the separate pieces to foam board (available at art supply shops) and hang with thumbtacks. A more elaborate version of this look would call for framing the separate pieces under glass.

Many lightbulbs are too stylish to be covered up with a lampshade. These long, narrow bulbs can even become a freeform chandelier when they are screwed into sockets and hung at different lengths over a dining table. This is the kind of unexpected touch that turns a traditional dining room into an eclectic—and electric—environment.

How-to: This is easiest when you have an overhead outlet. However, before you start, be sure to check with an electrician about wiring and safety guidelines for your particular situation.

A "chair railing" adds immediate architectural interest to a traditionally furnished room. The railing is a strip of molding that is nailed directly to the wall. This authentic colonial wall treatment gives you the opportunity to use a second color on the wall with the molding serving as a dividing strip.

How-to: Molding strips are available at most lumberyards. The strips range from ½-inch-wide plain semirounds to intricately carved 5-inch-wide cornices; prices are generally between 15¢ and $3.75 per foot, depending on thickness and style. Have the lumberyard cut the molding to size and use finishing nails twice the thickness of molding to attach it to the wall. Paint the molding with high-gloss enamel.

Chapter Four
Under $100

Why didn't someone think of this before? Wooden ladders can give you a pantry's worth of hanging space. No expensive hardware is needed. Hang the ladders from ropes or chains to hooks in the ceiling. You can hang the ladders either vertically or horizontally.

How-to: Before you hang heavy items from the ceiling, it's necessary to find your ceiling's beams. You can either do this by tapping the ceiling until you don't hear a hollow sound—or for extra assurance, you might buy a "stud finder" (available at hardware stores). Use long screws or butterfly bolts into the beams. Such screws are available with either hooks or eyes.

Large paintings have great style. Since artwork tends to be priced by the inch, the only way to get around the cost factor is by doing your own. The painting in the illustration was inspired by Jackson Pollack, who often took his canvases out to the backyard, spread them on the grass, and then proceeded to splatter them with different-colored acrylic paints. I've been told he walked over his paintings, rode a tricycle over them, and occasionally let some ashes drop on them. This sort of irrerence is fun to duplicate—and very effective.

How-to: Have canvas stretched to size at an art supply store, where you can also buy acrylic paints. It's important that the canvas be flat on the floor while you work (so the paint doesn't dribble). Try splattering the canvas from varying heights by standing first on a stool and then on a stepladder. Each height will give the paint a different texture and depth when it hits the canvas.

If your taste runs toward stark blocks of color, then you might let Mondrian, who is famous for his black-and-red box paintings, be an inspiration. Tape off the canvas into blocks and then paint in the colors of your choice. Pull the tape off when the paint is dry and you'll have a perfect white line.

When you have an old table that doesn't fit into the room or adds nothing decoratively, be bold and wrap it like a present. If you like the look when you have finished, then staple the fabric to the underpart of the legs of the table and add a ⅛-inch-thick tempered glass top or clear acrylic top.

The Japanese create floor designs with tatami mats. These are simple straw throw rugs with a binding of black fabric. These rugs can be sewn together to form interesting patterns, then taped to the floor with two-sided carpet tape to keep them from slipping. This type of finishing won't last forever, but it's an inexpensive way of giving a room an instant facelift.

•

Let the lighting become part of the decorating scheme. Inexpensive hanging fixtures take on a chic, offbeat look when used by the dozen. In addition to spreading a uniform light over a large space, they also have the effect of "lowering" the ceiling. Aluminum fixtures like the ones illustrated are available for less than $5 each.

Terra-cotta plumbing pipes used as planters or plant stands are ideal for city gardens. The pipes, which are available through plumbing supply companies, are sturdy and bring an out-doorsy look to an urban setting. In the illustration, pipes are used as plant stands. The saucers for the plants are balanced on the inner lip of the pipes.

How-to: To create a city garden for your plants and stands, use heavy-duty plastic drop cloth across the area where you will be watering plants. Cover the drop cloth with a layer of rocks or pebbles. Finally, arrange your plants at different heights using the terra-cotta pipes.

Use fabric pieces to make a quilt-patterned floor rug. Instead of being sewn together, as they would be for a quilt, the fabric pieces are glued to the floor. Like quilt-making itself, this calls for lots of patience. The pieces have to be cut first, then placed, and finally glued. After the glue has dried, they are then protected with four coats of polyurethane, which creates a hard finish.

How-to: The first step in creating a quilt-patterned floor is finding a good pattern book. There are several on the market. When you have found the right pattern, then start shopping for the cloth. Any inexpensive calico or patterned fabric will work here, but be sure to buy enough fabric. If you are doing a pattern that needs to be centered, start from the middle of the room and work outward toward the walls. Use a glue that's recommended for fabric and work with each piece very carefully (to be sure that it's smooth) before you go on to the next piece. Don't worry about frayed edges—you can clip them when the glue has dried.

Elegant ideas can come from the most unlikely sources. The room divider shown in the illustration was made from wire fencing. It's clamped at the top and bottom between two widths of wood. For a small room this is an ideal solution: It divides the space and yet leaves the room open visually. The fencing is available through fencing companies or in country stores.

How-to: Use pine or hardwood as clamps for base and ceiling. Measure the fencing carefully so the bottom boards will just barely reach the floor (to prevent buckling). To install the ceiling clamps: Use molly bolts with hooks that will slide into "eyes" screwed into the top boards. Attach the hooks on opposite boards as shown in the top-view illustration (left corner).

Another way to create an "open divider" is with a free-standing glass or steel bookcase. Keep only a few books and bibelots on the shelves for the best effect.

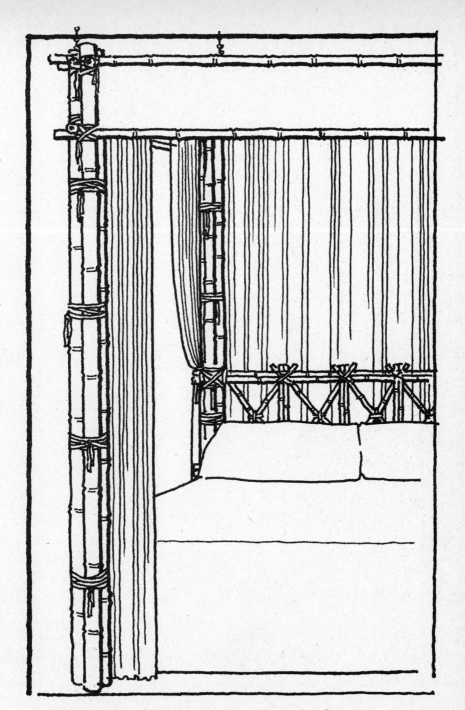

Bamboo can be tied together with silk cord to become a canopy frame and headboard. The look is glamorous and exotic, and the cost is minimal. To complete this tropical look, surround the bed with curtains made of sheer mosquito netting.

How-to: The bed frame shown in the illustration was put together in parts. Because it doesn't have lower supports, it would tilt if it weren't attached by a narrow chain to a ceiling hook. First, tie the bamboo posts into bundles and then tie the cross sections onto the posts. Raise the bed frame and chain it to the ceiling. Repeat this procedure for the headboard posts. Then tie on the sections that run the length of the bed. Now tie on the upper and lower cross sections that make the headboard and duplicate the pattern shown. If you want curtains, slip them onto the top posts before they are tied. (Mosquito netting is sold at camping supply shops.)

This bed takes some time to make—but it's a real knockout and well worth the effort.

Wish you owned a beautiful, ornate fireplace for those chilly winter nights? Well, a fun alternative is an enormous photograph of a fireplace. The one shown in the illustration was taken from a nineteenth-century architectural sketchbook. The cost of blowing up a 9 × 12-inch sheet to 4 × 6 feet is about $100. Photostat services are listed under *Photographic* in the Yellow Pages.

Industrial materials have residential chic when used in new and unexpected ways. For instance, the cardboard tubes in which cement is transported are perfect as columns, planters, storage units, and table bases. When the tubes are quartered lengthwise, they can be used to round the corners of walls, which softens the boxy architecture of high-rise apartment spaces.

How-to: The tubes can be sawed horizontally or vertically to size. For a finished look, paint tubes with two coats of high-gloss enamel. To find the tubes, look in the business phone directory under *Paper* and call the places that advertise tubes to do comparison shopping. Generally, a tube 8 inches across and 8 feet long is less than $25; a tube that is 16 inches across is less than $45.

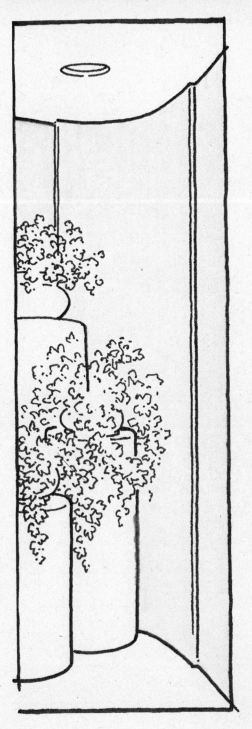

Instead of hanging a painting on the wall, display it on an easel.
The easels that artists use when they're painting have long
been used by galleries as a way of showing off artwork. The
price of the easel depends on the finish—the choice ranges
from raw wood to polished mahogany—but regardless of the
finish, an easel is a clever way of filling out a corner and making
a painting or print look like a masterpiece.

Finally! A headboard for people who love to read in bed and lean up against a cushy backing.

How-to: The headboard is a very heavy slab of dense foam cut to size. (You can find a source by looking under *Foam* in the Yellow Pages.) Cover the foam just as you would a pillow. Close it with Velcro so that it can be removed for cleaning or washing. Make straps holding the headboard to the rod detachable on the back with snaps. Use a brass or wooden rod that's at least 2 inches wide so it will have the proper thickness to complete the look. Rods are available in curtain departments.

Colorful glazed tiles make a spectacular-looking headboard. Tiles were a standard item in sultans' palaces—and they can be a part of your life with this simple-to-construct patterned headboard. This is a first-rate solution for decorating a small bedroom, where the addition of a typical headboard might simply add clutter.

How-to: Tiling is a cinch if you're dealing with flat walls in good condition. Use self-adhesive tiles or regular tiles that can be caulked to the wall. (Caulking is available at hardware stores; look for tiles wherever linoleum is sold.) If you're working out a pattern, lay it out on the floor first, or diagram it using graph paper. After installing the tiles, either paint the wall in a matching or harmonizing color or, for added effect, wallpaper the area with a paper that picks up the tile colors.

What to do with a window that faces a wall? Hang a rectangular sheet of plastic that is the same color as the wall in front of the window. This way, you will get the light and be able to open the window, and yet not be faced with a boring view. Stores that sell such plastic will cut it to size and also drill holes to hang it from.

Louvered slats give you a graceful way to cover a radiator. This is an ideal treatment for high-rise apartments.

How-to: Nail together a frame wide and deep enough to cover the radiator. Nail small blocks of wood to the frame to serve as guides for the slanted plywood. Top the unit with a plywood shelf and paint to match the walls.

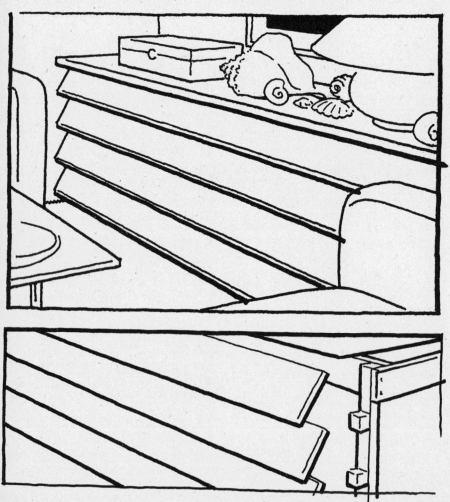

For small spaces where you sometimes want privacy, hang venetian blinds or matchstick shades. They are less expensive to install than a wall and more practical—they can be pulled up when you want to "open" the room. Blinds are available in many colors and it will be easy to find a shade that matches or blends with your walls.

How-to: Venetian blinds come with all the hardware necessary to hang them directly from the ceiling.

Think of felt when you want a fabric-covered wall. Felt is available in a full palette of colors, and its soft, warm texture makes it an ideal wall covering that's easily installed with a staple gun. Or consider felt as a bedspread in a modern bedroom. Felt wraps neatly to create a sleek look, and it's inexpensive enough so that you can afford a wardrobe or different bedspreads.

For extra dash, make a wall mural. Using simple shapes, you can create a museum-worthy work of art with scissors, staples, and glue.

How-to: Next to paper, felt is the easiest material to work with. It can be cut with scissors and doesn't need a hem. The usual width of the material is 72 inches, which means that it can be used to cover large areas without being seamed. It lends itself to being stapled, thumbtacked, or glued to any surface.

Staple the first layer of fabric to the wall. Trim it neatly at the ceiling and floor with a razor. Use a length of brown paper or newspaper taped together to make your patterns for the trees and mountains shown here. Glue the second layer of felt to the first layer.

●

Some of the top English decorators are quite famous for mixing inexpensive industrial materials with antiques. One of their favorite choices of wall covering is brown corrugated cardboard. The color and texture serve as a pleasing background for furnishings of any period. Corrugated board is available by the sheet (a 36 × 48-inch piece is about $1.75) at office supply stores; but if you're going to need a lot of it, call the source—packaging suppliers.

Make your entranceway shine with pure Art Deco elegance: a classic '20s look is translated easily and inexpensively with mirror squares. Consider this treatment for a dining room, too. Against dark-colored walls, the diagonally placed mirrors sparkle like diamonds and create a gem of a setting!

How-to: Mirror squares are backed with a very effective contact glue, which means that once the squares are in place they can't be moved around. Plan your pattern carefully before you start, and work slowly. The results are spectacular and well worth the effort. If your pattern is to be centered, then start from that spot and work outward. Squares can be cut with a mirror cutter, which is available at most paint stores or wherever you buy the squares.

The brass-edged closet mirrors that you see at the dime store for less than $15 each look handsome when they are lined up side by side over a sofa. You can also find these mirrors with wood edges. The wood can be painted the same color as your wall, which will give the mirrors the look of built-in panels.

The beams in a country kitchen add an earthy texture to the room and also serve as a hanging gallery for pretty baskets, lanterns, and plants. You can capture the look with Styrofoam beams. They come prefinished and will hold to the ceiling with a contact glue. If you are planning to hang heavy items from the beams, they'll have to be more carefully installed.

How-to: The Styrofoam beams are U-shaped with hollow insides. Measure the U and screw a matching strip of wood to the ceiling. (The wood should be screwed into the crossbeams in your own ceiling.) Then screw the Styrofoam beams onto the wood supports.

●

Turn an undistinguished item of furniture into a handsome piece with handpainted glazed tiles. These tiles tend to be expensive ($3 to $10 or more each) but they are charming and well worth the investment if you're only covering a small piece. Glue the tiles down carefully on an absolutely clean and dry surface; the tile shop will sell you the fixative.

Ready-made mirrored plant stands are often less expensive than those you can make yourself. These cubes come in a variety of heights. Look for a small one to use as a coffee table or end table; use taller ones to hold sculpture, plants, or vases of flowers.

Want to bring some sunshine into a dark and dreary room? When window reveals are mirrored, the effect is to increase the light as it reflects off the mirrors. This makes it an ideal treatment for small windows as well as windows with a northern exposure. A side benefit of mirrored reveals is that they offer glimpses of the outdoors from unusual angles.

How-to: See illustration for placement of the mirrors, then measure your window reveals to determine the size of mirrors you will need. A mirror shop will cut mirroring to size. Finally, attach with a sturdy glue.

By using 2 × 2-inch strips of wood that have been precut at the lumberyard, you can stack and nail a coffee-table base. The table in the illustration is unbleached oak, but it would also be very attractive lacquered a high-gloss black, red, or white.

How-to: Before you start, sand the ends of the wood so they're smooth and attractive. Stack the strips log-cabin-style by first placing two in one direction and then placing the cross strips in the opposite direction. Nail the strips together and add the next section until the table is the right height. Then turn the table over and there will be no nails showing on the bottom section. To keep the glass top from sliding, it's always a good idea to use small rubber rounds (available at any hardware store) on the corners of the base.

Note: Whenever buying glass for a tabletop, always be sure it's tempered glass, which is heat resistant.

A terra-cotta planter becomes an earthy coffee-table base when it's topped with a round of glass. The best sources for oversized planters are shops that sell trees. Tempered glass tops are available in a wide variety of sizes and depths, or you can have glass cut to size by a glazier. Glass is heavy and you should inquire whether the base you're using will support the width and size glass that you have selected.

Sisal rugs are one of the great furnishing bargains. They are sometimes referred to as "straw rugs," but sisal is actually a plant which many peoples have been weaving into floor coverings for generations. Many sisal rugs are still made by hand and often have interesting patterns. Sisal rugs give rooms a beach-house look. They aren't as durable as fabric rugs, but they will last longer if laid over a thin rubber backing. For small rugs, you can find a 3 × 5-foot foam backing at the dime store for less than $5. Larger rubber mats are available at carpeting shops. Buy the least expensive type of foam—sisal won't last forever, no matter what type of backing you have. The best place to shop for sisal rugs is in the oriental import shops, where a 6 × 9-foot size might be in the $75-or-less range.

You can give a sisal rug an unexpected twist by painting on it. Sisal rugs lend themselves to this treatment because the design is already woven in and all you have to do is follow the pattern. For instance, you could paint the borders light yellow and half the triangles a deep rose.

How-to: You can use any kind of paint (oil-base or water-base), but it should be thinned by 10% to 25% with turpentine so the paint will go into all the little crevices. Use a fine brush that can be wedged into the straw. Try one section first to make sure the paint is thin enough and dries the right color on the sisal.

Any piece of furniture with a scratched or marred top can be given an instant facelift with a new mirrored top cut to size and finished by a glazier.

Inexpensive patterned rugs can become dramatic artwork when they are hung as tapestries. Abstract patterns and unusual colorations are the trademark of the rugs of many cultures that have long practiced rugmaking as a highly prized art form. These rugs are available at most department stores, but the most interesting and offbeat patterns are often found in shops that specialize in the crafts of a nation. Shop around for Indian, Turkish, Mexican, Peruvian, and Afghan rugs. Many of these are one of a kind and surprisingly good buys for the amount of hand craftsmanship that is involved.

How-to: When hanging rugs as art, tack a thin strip of wood to the wall at the top of the rug and then tack the rug to the wood. This will hold the rug securely without damaging it.

There isn't always smoke where there's fire. A nonworking fireplace becomes a handsome focal point when it's lined with mirrored squares and lit with hurricane lamps. With mirrors on three sides, the flame from the lamps is reflected to infinity, creating an inviting glow any time of the year. Brass hurricane lamps use kerosene as fuel, which is available at most hardware stores. Hurricane lamps are attractive accessories on end tables or in the dining room. They give off a very soft, romantic light. Best of all, you don't need an open flue when using hurricane lamps.

Signal for style: The signal flags used on boats are called sema-phore flags. They are ideal as upbeat, bold wall hangings. Available at marine supply shops.

Canvas-covered pillows and mattresses are given instant cheer with handpainted stripes of pink and yellow. Don't worry if the stripes are less than perfect or if a bit of the paint is dripped—the look is meant to be casual and impetuous. Canvas is a heavy-duty fabric and looks best in sunrooms, casual living rooms, and kids' rooms. It's still one of the best buys around. You can find 54-inch-wide canvas for less than $5 per yard in most stores. Shown in the illustration are canvas-covered throw pillows and a mattress.

How-to: See page 73 for information on painting the canvas covered chair.

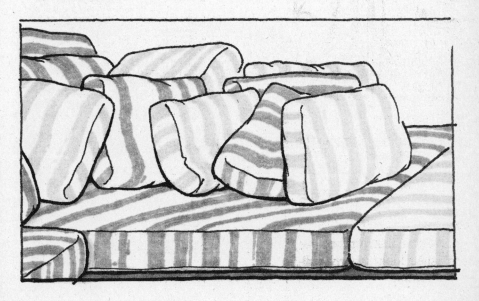

Chapter Five
Under $200

If storage space is one of your biggest problems, here's an ideal solution: matchstick shades on either side of a bureau to turn dead space into a storage wall. Matchstick shades make this a very economical treatment: 6 × 6-foot matchstick shades are generally less than $30 at oriental import shops.

How-to: To create walls on either side of the dresser, use plywood that's anchored at the floor and ceiling with L-shaped brackets. This will make the "wall" strong enough to support shelves. If you aren't going to build in shelves, then it would be easier and less expensive to use wallboard. The matchstick shades are hung from the ceiling with small hooks.

Although matchstick shades are an ideal way of covering walls that are in poor condition, many decorators use them as a wall-covering simply because they create such a tropical-looking environment. This is an especially attractive treatment for rooms with lots of plants and casual furniture. The shades are hung with cuphooks.

Bands of pattern add an elegant touch to traditional decor. Use wallpaper borders (which are 2- or 3-inch-wide strips that can be bought separately from wallpaper) to outline windows, doors, or walls. Spend some time browsing in a wallpaper store. You'll be delighted with the wide range of borders for every room of the house—there are fruit patterns for the kitchen, flowers for the bedroom, and tartan plaids for a child's room.

How-to: Many border prints are prepasted. However, even the regular rolls are easy to handle and install with wallpaper paste. Woodwork is usually the guideline for installation, but if you want to place the border below the ceiling or away from the woodwork for aesthetic reasons, don't hesitate. You're adding decoration and you don't need to follow any rules.

Looking for an unusual window treatment to use on apartment windows? Canvas panels that slide open and closed on a track are interesting. The panels can be pushed completely open during the day to allow in the light and closed in the evening to show off a handpainted design.

How-to: Buy track cut to size at a lumberyard. Buy canvas panels at an art supply store; the store will make the panels to size. You will be buying the kind of canvas that artists use: It will have a wood frame and the canvas will be tightly stapled around it. The design shown in the illustration was made by taping the triangular outline onto the canvas and then painting within the tape.

Borrow a look from English country houses and hang curtains at the corners of your bed to create a very luxurious hideaway. The curtains in the illustration were made from a solid sheeting and a patterned sheeting.

How-to: Hang drapery hardware at the corners. Sew the sheets to "drapery tape," which is available in notions shops. The tape will automatically pleat the fabric.

For a studio apartment, a second bedroom, or any space where you need the bed to double as a seating area, use felt to cover the bed and make pillows to match. Felt is durable, easy to work with, inexpensive, and available in a full palette of colors.

How-to: The rainbow pillows shown in the illustration are dense foam, which is bought from a shop which specializes in this material. A foam specialist will cut it to size for you and advise you on the proper density and thickness for your project. (For a source, look under *Foam* in the Yellow Pages.) To make the pillow covers, first cut a pattern out of newspaper. Allow 1 inch for seams. The bedspread and box-spring cover can either be seamed at the corners or tightly wrapped with "hospital corners."

The updated version of the "storage box" is a seating unit with a hinged top. It's a perfect small-place solution because it gives the impression of being a piece of custom furniture, while it enables you to store out-of-season clothing, extra suitcases, and items that aren't used regularly. Unless you're handy, have the unit built by a carpenter so that it will be sturdy and well finished.

The luxurious version of this: Cover the base and top with material that matches the pillows. Staple cotton batting to the wood before covering in order to give a rounded, soft look. Or, instead of yard goods, buy a quilt and use that as the covering for the base and pillows. Because of the excellent buys at white sales, one can often find beautiful quilts that are better buys than quilted fabric in the yard-goods department.

Extra closet space may be as hard to come by in this world as money! Here's an ideal solution for achieving loads of extra space and adding a decorative element as well: Create a corner closet that requires no wall construction by installing curtains to close off a storage area.

How-to: Hang curtain rods at right angles. Choose a curtain fabric that matches your sheets or window coverings. Install shelves with standards and brackets from the hardware store.

Create a distinguished-looking wall by using molding strips to frame colorful maps. Secondhand bookshops often have old maps that aren't quite antique but are more interesting than new maps. These maps are generally less than $5 each. You can also find handsome copies of antique maps.

How-to: It's easiest to stain molding strips before they are nailed to the wall. For a traditional look, use a mahogany stain. The brass decorations are available at specialty hardware stores. They are nailed onto the corners after the strips have been installed. Make sure that walls are clean and perfectly smooth before gluing up maps. If map edges overlap molding, trim with a razor.

Moving pads have moved out of vans and into the living room. The pads are being updated for consumers. Instead of "mover's gray," you can find fuchsia, red, bright blue, or tawny beige. They're cotton, which means they are washable, durable, and easy to work with. In the illustration, a multilevel platform takes on a custom look and is comfortable and inviting when covered with moving pads. Attach the pads with thumbtacks so they can be removed for machine washing. A layer of foam rubber softens the seating area. (To construct a platform, you will need to consult a good carpentry book for directions.) Ask your local mover where to buy the pads. A 96 × 76-inch pad costs less than $25.

Mylar makes a beautiful covering for a Parsons table or an old, undistinguished piece of furniture. Wrap the Mylar around the table and staple neatly. To give the wrap an expensive look, use brass or silver upholsterer's tacks at the corners and down the table legs. These tacks are available at notions shops.

Make your bathroom glamorous by mirroring the ceiling. It creates the impression of a double-height room and makes even the smallest bathroom feel twice as large. Mylar, the silvery plastic that looks like mirror, creates the same effect. In the illustration shown, Mylar was stapled to a trellis to create a doubly interesting finish. (You can also "mirror" bathroom walls with Mylar. A 27-inch-wide roll that is 15 feet long costs about $14.)

How-to: Unframed trellis is available at lumberyards and nurseries. Frame the trellis with strips of plywood. Paint it. Staple the Mylar to the edges of the frame. Put hooks on the part of the frame that faces the ceiling and put hook eyes into the ceiling. Hook the frame to the eyes.

Mirror strips give stairways a high-stepping elegance! It's easy to install the strips on the risers.

How-to: Take measurements to a mirror shop and have mirror strips cut to size. Buy the proper glue for installing the mirror from the shop.

Turn an extra closet into a study area with a tabletop and
shelves. The closet workspace can be elaborate or simple. The
easiest-to-install desk is a slab of wood or Formica supported on
one side by a two-drawer steel file cabinet and on the other side
by a cleat nailed to the wall. For added glamour, install mirroring on the back wall and use glass shelves to complement the
mirroring. For the closet to be truly useful as a workspace, it
needs to be lit from within. Clamp lamps that clip onto the
shelves will work; or for a more finished look, use the wall-
mounted can lights shown in the illustration.

You'll feel like a pampered princess in a Hollywood-style bed. The padding and pleating make it comfortable to lean against, and if you use sheets that match your comforter or pillow, you'll increase the dramatic effect.

How-to: Cut ½-inch plywood with a saber saw. (Unless you have experience with tools, you should have a professional do this.) Smooth three layers of cotton batting across the front and staple at the back. Shop for batting at the dime store. Mark the bottom center of the headboard and staple fabric to this point. Pull fabric from center to the outside edges in 2-inch pleats. The center area will look messy, but this doesn't matter, because the lower portion of the headboard will be below the mattress level. Edge the top with grosgrain ribbon. Bolt the headboard to the wall with heavy screws across the lower portion that is covered by the mattress.

Put your plants on display by creating a gardening area in your living room with ceramic tile. Just lay the tiles down over a hardwood floor or carpet. (There's no need to attach the tiles to the floor unless you'll be walking on them.) Now you won't have to worry about water stains on your floor or dirt on your carpet. But best of all, the tiles will add a look of luxury and style to your house.

How-to: To prevent the tiles from slipping, go to a carpet store and purchase a thin rubber mat. Place the mat beneath the tiles.

Cover your floors and walls with the same substance used to cover diving boards—cocoa matting. Cocoa matting is ideal for modern rooms because it adds texture without detracting from the sleek look of the furnishings. Matting 48 inches wide is available at swimming pool suppliers for less than $5 per yard.

Mosquito netting adds sheer allure to an easily assembled canopy and glamorizes a small bedroom. Mosquito netting is available by the yard at camping supply stores.

How-to: Have two dowels cut to size at the lumberyard. Rest the dowels on a ring that is attached to a chain hanging from a hook and eye in the ceiling. The mosquito netting is pulled over the dowels. When buying netting, allow for at least 18 inches of extra fabric for the canopy to drape gracefully.

Cover an ugly attic ceiling with yards of gathered fabric. If you're lucky enough to have an attic or a top floor with a slanted ceiling and wood beams, then you have the ideal backdrop for creating the look shown in the illustration, where wires and ugly insulating materials are covered by curtained panels.

How-to: Buy fabric twice the width of each panel so that it can be gathered fully on curtain rods. If you are installing the panels in small areas, then you can use tension rods that snap into place and hold sturdily.

Industrial chic: Steel footlockers are an ideal way to create a colorful, practical, instantly finished storage wall. The lockers come in white, chrome yellow, and industrial green. You can price them by looking under *Lockers* in the Yellow Pages.

Curtained walls look terrific in any room, but they give a special elegance and feeling of luxury when used in a bedroom. Consider using bed sheets for the curtains. Bed sheets come in so many great patterns, and the coordinated effect you'll achieve by matching your bedroom linen to your walls will be sensational.

How-to: Hem fabric top and bottom. (If you use bed sheets, you won't have to bother with this step.) Be sure the measurements are accurate so your fabric doesn't sag. There is no need to seam the fabric, as the edges will be concealed in the fullness. Finally, install the "curtains" on the wall as you would in a window with rods and curtain hardware.

Were the classically styled columns shown in the illustration built centuries ago? Did they cost a fortune? The answer to both questions is an emphatic *no*! These columns were built by a carpenter from ordinary plywood, and the moldings—which give the column their "look" —are from the lumberyard and cost less than $1 per foot.

How-to: The columns are long boxes made from four pieces of wood with a hollow inner core. Unless you're very handy, have a carpenter build them so the edges are matched perfectly. Nail on molding strips after column is built.

Here's a clever way to give your dining room a country look. Have a carpenter build a display shelf built in the same sturdy design used by colonial craftsmen. You'll have a perfect place for showing off breakable treasures, such as china or porcelain vases.

Mirror squares topped with a strip of molding turn an ordinary room into a traditional masterpiece. This treatment works equally well in an entrance foyer, living room, or dining area. It's especially appropriate for rooms with a formal decorating scheme.

How-to: Use self-adhesive mirror squares, which can be bought at most paint or housewares stores. If any of the squares need to be cut, buy a mirror-cutting knife where you buy the squares. As a finishing touch, nail a strip of molding (available at lumberyards) over the top of the mirrors.

Chapter Six
Under $300

We tend to think of wainscotting as a farmhouse look—which it was until savvy city dwellers saw the advantage of installing it in their homes to create a country look. Wainscotting works best with informal furniture—either pine, wicker, or a casual mixture of furnishings. With wainscotting, consider accessories like rag rugs, brass kerosene lamps, and old-fashioned hunting prints on the wall.

How-to: Yellow pine wainscotting is available for about 55¢ per linear foot (3½ inches wide) and it can be precut to length at the lumberyard. Install with long thin nails. Across the top of the wainscotting, use a strip of molding to give it a finished look. The wainscotting can either be painted a traditional white or stained to match your woodwork.

Platform beds and seating areas are an ideal solution for smallish rooms. The low, neat look of a platform makes a room seem larger and less cluttered than it might appear with conventional furniture. The cost of building in a platform is usually less than the cost of buying comparable furniture and it gives you the added advantage of custom-designing the unit to suit your needs and the size of your room.

If the platform is to be covered with carpeting, then the least expensive way to build it is by using utility-grade lumber. This is lumber with imperfections—but imperfections don't matter under carpeting, and such lumber can be as much as 25% cheaper than higher-grade wood. When buying carpeting for a platformed room, be sure to tell the salesman about the platform, because the vertical surfaces necessitate additional carpeting.

Building a platform on an angle saves space and creates interest. The platform shown in the illustration has a triangular backrest in the corner which opens at the top and serves as a storage space for blankets and extra pillows.

How-to: A platform needs to be built by a professional carpenter, or by an amateur who knows what he or she is doing. Don't attempt a platform without reading a carpentry book that supplies plans and directions.

A tented ceiling is romantic in a small dining area or bedroom. The style comes from the exotic East, where swagged fabric, big pillows, and rich dark colors are the decorating staples. For tenting, you can use any lightweight patterned fabric. This is a good place for a paisley pattern that might be too busy if it were hung on the wall.

How-to: Measure the room carefully and buy enough fabric for twice the width of the room (so that it can be gathered and not look skimpy). Seam all the fabric together. To make the swag, on the back of the fabric sew a 2-inch-wide binding ribbon at each place that you want the fabric to drape. The binding ribbon will create the pocket for the curtain rod. Gather material on the rod. Hang the rods on cup hooks screwed into the ceiling. You may need several hooks for each swag so the rod doesn't sag.

Secretarial chairs work as well at home as in the office. These chairs are being widely used by top New York decorators who specialize in very modern rooms. Consider the secretarial chairs for a small dining corner or alcove where bigger chairs might crowd the space.

Old bathrooms lend themselves to whimsical, romantic decorating. The not-so-splendid fixtures seem like an asset when they are treated to quick cosmetic tricks, such as adding skirts to cover their stained sides and too-visible plumbing. Go one step further and look for ways to turn the bathroom into a pretty-as-a-parlor place: Make curtains to match the wallpaper, look for new lighting fixtures, and use colorful rag rugs instead of the standard bathmat. Bathrooms are fun to decorate because they are small and the cost is much less than it would be for a living room or bedroom.

How-to: Skirt a bathtub or sink with fabric sewn to a Velcro band. Glue the other side of the band to the sink with a contact glue. Velcro is a fabric "zipper" that allows you to remove the skirt for washing. It's available at dime stores and fabric shops.

If you're serious about your gardening, explore the possibility of a window greenhouse. Many are available for less than $300 and are sized for standard windows. These structures give plants the benefit of the best possible light—and give you the luxury of an out-of-the-way garden. Look under *Greenhouses* in the Yellow Pages. There are also many advertisements in the back of shelter magazines, such as *House Beautiful* and *House & Garden*. Send away for catalogues and compare prices, ease of installation, and size.

Flokati rugs are glamorous and inviting and give the same effect as fur for a lot less money. Flokati is a wool and can be tub-washed; it's practical, durable, and very showy. Use it either as a rug or as a bed covering. A 6 × 9-foot size is about $250.

Trellis can be beautiful when used as a headboard and footboard in a country-style bedroom or in a little girl's room. One scheme: Paint the trellis white and paint the walls of the room a deep blue; use a rag rug on the floor and a white comforter and white pillows on the bed.

Trellis also makes an excellent wall covering when painted. It's particularly useful over bad walls. Paint the wall a contrasting color for a three-dimensional look.

Use trellis across one wall in the kitchen and hang pots and pans from it. Try painting it a bright red for a cheerful look.

Photorealism: an enlargement of a photograph used as a wall-to-wall mural. You can use your own photos or professional photos. Museum gift shops are a great resource for slides: There's no reason you shouldn't live with a wall-size photo of a Picasso or Rubens. In most tourist centers, slides are as readily available as postcards.

Make a small dining room look twice its size by mirroring an entire wall. For the best effect, place your dining-room table directly against the mirrored wall. This way, your table will look twice as long too!

Chapter Seven
Under $500

The mirrored screen shown in the illustration was installed in the corner of an elegant Manhattan penthouse apartment because the owners were desperately short of storage space. Instead of building an extra closet, they opted for the mirror screen, which is built on casters so that it can be rolled out of the way. Hidden behind this elegant screen is a washer-dryer, extra shelves for out-of-season clothes, and tax records that would clutter their regular closets. Who would believe that you could so cleverly conceal a washer-dryer in your living room?

How-to: This screen can be made with doors that are mirror-covered. However, the weight of the mirrors can unbalance an imperfectly constructed screen, and you might be wiser to seek out a mirror shop that will build the screen to your specifications. It's worth the extra cost to have a screen that you can use for a lifetime.

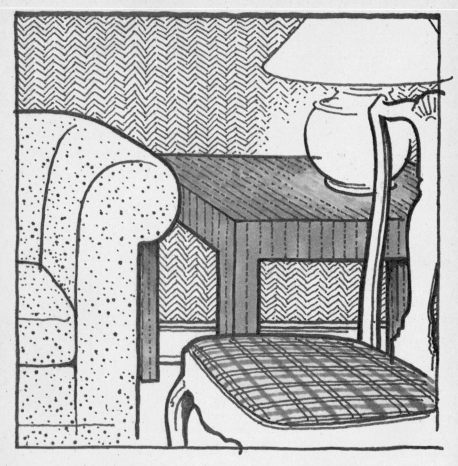

For sheer luxury, almost nothing beats a fur rug. Although many department stores sell fur rugs, the best place to get a good buy is at a furrier. Quite often, furriers will have 44 × 88-inch rugs that are made of scraps. Thus, you can get some of the moxt luxurious furs—mink, fox, even ermine—for a fraction of what you'd expect to pay. My own favorite fur blanket is mole. Mole is relatively inexpensive (less than $500) and looks like the richest velvet when it's dyed burgundy or royal blue. Any fur can be dyed to match your color scheme. The dyers charge by the pound, so the lighter-weight furs, such as mink, are better furs to dye than heavier furs, such as fox.

Men's suiting fabrics have become one of the most fashionable upholstery materials. A subtle tweed, charcoal gray, or cream flannel is beautiful for a sofa; plaid material is smart for accent pieces, such as a chair seat or stool covering; and herringbone tweeds or pinstripes are handsome and unexpected on the walls.

Instead of a glass top or wood top for a table, consider marble. It's always elegant and special-looking. There are as many grades of marble as there are of diamonds and precious stones. And just as most gemstones are lovely to the naked eye, so is most marble. Marble is graded according to rarity, closeness to perfection, thickness, and size. Some of the least expensive marbles are simply beautiful.

Overhead fans bring recollections of old Sidney Greenstreet movies and the aristocratic South. Many decorators have used them for years because they have such a good "look." But there's an added benefit: They can cut your air-conditioning bill in the summer and lower your heating bill in the winter by circulating the cold or warm air. Fans range in price from about $220 to $500, depending on style and finish. With 8-foot ceilings, a white steel fan might have a crisp look; in a room with high ceilings, a wood fan with heavy paddles would be an excellent choice.

•

Ornamental ceilings and decorative woodwork add great charm to any room—but since most of us aren't lucky enough to move into a place with elegant medallions on the ceiling or splendid woodwork, the next best thing is to buy it. Fortunately, the renewed interest in restoration has created many new sources for plaster casts and metal copies of these lovely old pieces.

If you're lucky enough to be able to spare a closet in the den or living room, then you have a perfect setting for a glamorous mirrored bar. With a small refrigerator or cabinet below, the bar makes entertaining easier and adds a stylish element to the room.

Porch swings are fun indoors—and add a totally unexpected, casual look to any living room. You can sometimes find used porch swings at auctions and secondhand shops in the country. (Warning: Installing a heavy object calls for savvy—or an expert.)

Shoji screens are the classic Japanese window coverings and room dividers. They are made with rice paper that is wedged between narrow strips of ebony or blond wood to create a grid pattern. Shoji screens are relatively expensive (because of the amount of hand workmanship required), but they are an ideal solution for rooms without a view. The rice paper allows the light to filter in and yet provides complete privacy.

Pressed metal ceilings were widely used in restaurants and industrial buildings in the '30s. The silvery finish and embossed patterns have proved to be an ideal low-maintenance material, as well as being decorative and inexpensive. It's only recently, however, that designers and architects have seen their potential for residential use on walls. The embossed metal comes in 2 × 8-foot strips that are about $10 each. The metal is thin and difficult to handle, and it's recommended that it be professionally installed. To comparison-price the metal and installation costs, look in the Yellow Pages under *Ceilings—Metal*.

Bibliography

Basic Carpentry Techniques, T.J. Williams, Ortho Books, 1981.

Bed and Bath Book, Terence Conran, Crown, 1978

Better Homes and Garden: Your Walls and Ceilings, Meredith, 1983.

The Carpenter's Manifesto, Jeffrey Ehrlich and Marc Manheimer,
    Holt Rinehart and Winston, 1977.

De Cristoforo's Complete Book of Power Tools, R. J. De Cristoforo,
    Harper & Row, 1972.

Fundamentals of Carpentry, Walter Durbahn and Robert E. Putnam,
    American Technical Society, 1977.

The House Book, Terence Conran, Crown, 1974.

How to Work with Tools and Wood, Robert Campbell and
    N.H. Mager, Pocket Books, 1975.

Reader's Digest Complete Do-It-Yourself Manual, Reader's Digest
    Assn., Inc., 1981.

Woodworking and Furnituremaking, G. W. Endacott,
    Drake Publishers, 1972.

Titles of Related Interest from PLUME